DATE DUE

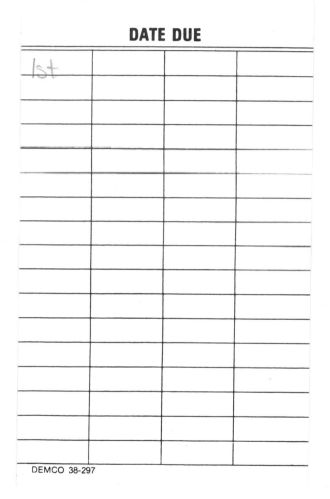

1st			

DEMCO 38-297

PILGRIMS
and
THANKSGIVING

Troll Associates

PILGRIMS
and
THANKSGIVING

by Rae Bains

Illustrated by David Wenzel

Troll Associates

Library of Congress Cataloging in Publication Data

Bains, Rae.
    Pilgrims and Thanksgiving.

    Summary: Briefly traces the history of the Pilgrims,
a group of Puritans who fled England to escape religious
persecution, sailed to Massachusetts on the Mayflower,
and celebrated their first harvest there in 1621 with
a great feast.
    1. Pilgrims (New Plymouth colony)—Juvenile literature.
2. Thanksgiving Day—Juvenile literature. 3. Massachusetts—History—New Plymouth, 1620-1691—Juvenile
literature. [1. Pilgrims (New Plymouth colony)
2. Thanksgiving Day. 3. Massachusetts—History—
New Plymouth, 1620-1691] I. Wenzel, David,
1950-   ill. II. Title.
F68.B134   1984   973.2′2   84-2686
ISBN 0-8167-0222-5 (lib. bdg.)
ISBN 0-8167-0223-3 (pbk.)

It is the year 1620. More than a hundred people are crowded aboard a small wooden sailing ship called the *Mayflower*. They have spent more than two months crossing the angry Atlantic. Their destination is the Virginia Colony. There, they hope to find a better life than they had in England. Some seek wealth. Others seek adventure. Still others, called *Separatists*, seek freedom to worship as they please.

At last, land is sighted. The ship sails around a sandy cape and into a large bay. But something is wrong. This is not the Virginia Colony. They are much too far north. By accident, the Pilgrims have reached Massachusetts instead of Virginia!

The religious problems that brought many of the Pilgrims to the New World had been building for a long time. Almost a century earlier, King Henry VIII had broken away from the Roman Catholic Church and established the Anglican Church—the Church of England.

But many people in England felt he had not gone far enough with church reform. They said that the Church of England was still too much like the Catholic Church.

These religious reformers did not approve of what they felt were the showy rituals of the Anglican Church. They did not approve of the church government. Because they wanted to purify the church, they were called *Puritans*.

They believed that each group of worshipers should be free to choose its own minister. They believed that everyone was equal before God, and that reading the Bible and obeying the Ten Commandments were the foundation stones of faith.

Some Puritans hoped to reform the Church of England. Others did not believe that the church could ever be persuaded to change. So they formed their own separate congregation outside the established church. These people were the Separatists.

The Separatists suffered harsh conditions under the British government. They could not attend universities. They could not worship openly. Some were thrown into jail. Others were condemned to death.

Many Separatists left England to escape this persecution. A number of them went to the Netherlands, where they could worship freely. Among the Separatists was a group from a northern English village called Scrooby. This group, which left England in 1608, spent several years in the city of Leiden in the Netherlands.

Most of the Scrooby Separatists were farmers, and they were not happy living in the city. Those who were craftsmen were not happy either. They were not allowed to join the guilds, or Dutch trade groups.

Some of the Separatists from Scrooby became sailors aboard Dutch merchant ships. Their children began to speak and act like Dutch children, instead of English children. The Separatist leaders saw that their numbers were growing smaller, and they grew increasingly concerned. Finally, they decided to leave the Netherlands.

From the Netherlands, they returned to England in 1620. From there, they planned to sail across the Atlantic to the Virginia Colony. In America, they hoped to retain their English identity and to find religious freedom as well. It was this group, then, that formed the core of the Pilgrims who would travel to America.

In England, they recruited a number of other people, whom they called the Strangers, to go with them. There were approximately eighty Strangers, who were not Separatists or Puritans. They included Captain Miles Standish, John Alden, and the young woman whom Alden would later marry—Priscilla Mullens.

The Strangers were not going to the New World for religious reasons. Some wanted to improve their lives, some were seeking adventure, and some were hoping to make their fortunes.

The members of the group obtained a charter to settle in the Virginia Colony. Two ships, the *Speedwell* and the *Mayflower*, were outfitted for the Atlantic crossing. Several London merchants agreed to finance the voyage. The merchants hoped to profit from the huge catches of fish the Pilgrims expected to take from the waters off the Virginia coast.

Twice during that summer, the two ships set sail, and twice they had to return to port. Both times it was because the *Speedwell* proved unseaworthy.

At last, on September 6, 1620, the *Mayflower* set sail alone from Plymouth, England. It was a rough crossing for the heavily laden, ninety-foot wooden ship. Autumn gales in the Atlantic and faulty maps took the travelers north of the Virginia Colony.

After sixty-six danger-filled days at sea, the *Mayflower* dropped anchor in Provincetown Harbor at the point of Cape Cod, Massachusetts. The date was November 21, 1620.

The Pilgrims were happy to reach shore, but concerned that they had not landed in the Virginia Colony. Their charter—and the arrangement with the London merchants—had been for Virginia. Some of the Strangers talked about breaking away. They said that since this was not Virginia, they were free to do as they pleased.

The Pilgrim leaders saw that this attitude could lead to trouble, so a document was written that set the rules of their new colony. This document, known as the Mayflower Compact, said that the settlers would draw up their own just and equal laws for the good of all the members of the new colony.

The Mayflower Compact was signed, and John Carver was elected governor. This made him the first freely elected colonial governor in the New World.

For the next month, the Pilgrims used the *Mayflower* as their base while they explored the coast along Cape Cod Bay. The place they finally chose for their settlement was Plymouth. It had a brook with good drinking water, a hill where they could build a fort, and farm fields.

A map the Pilgrims used showed that there had once been an Indian village at Plymouth. The Indians had been wiped out by a deadly disease called smallpox. But the farm lands they had cleared were in good condition for planting.

The Pilgrims' first winter in the New World was a harsh one. The cold and snow, combined with sickness and a dwindling food supply, reduced the colony's population from 101 people to about half that many.

But spring and planting time brought the promise of better days. It also brought a surprise. One day, an Indian brave entered the settlement. His first words, introducing himself and welcoming the Pilgrims, were in English. This stunned and delighted the winter-weary, discouraged settlers.

The Indian, whose name was Samoset, told the Pilgrims that he had learned their language from English sailors and traders. He told them about the countryside and about the Indian tribes in the area. They were all friendly, he said, and the Pilgrims had nothing to fear from them.

A few days later, Samoset brought another Indian, named Squanto, to meet the Pilgrims. Squanto was a member of the tribe that had once lived at Plymouth.

Squanto became the settlers' friend, guide, and teacher. He taught the Pilgrims how to catch fish and eels, how to plant corn, how to use fish for fertilizer in the fields, and where to find herbs in the forest. He showed the Pilgrims which wild plants were good to eat. And he taught them many other valuable lessons about their new home.

Through Squanto, who acted as an interpreter, the Pilgrims met the great chief Massasoit and made a treaty with his tribe, the Wampanoag Indians of southeastern Massachusetts.

The treaty pledged that each side would cause no harm to the other. It promised that an Indian who injured a settler would face the settlers' justice, and that a settler who injured an Indian would face Indian justice. In addition, the settlers and Indians promised to defend each other against all enemies.

The Pilgrims devoted the spring and summer of 1621 to planting, tending the crops, hunting and trading with the Indians, and making the settlement more secure and comfortable. By the end of the summer, the village had a sturdy Common House (for meetings and worship), some storehouses, and several wooden homes along a single street.

The Pilgrims' homes were one-room cabins with walls made of boards and roofs made of thatch. There was a large stone fireplace to provide warmth, heat for cooking, and light. The room was cluttered with rough furniture, barrels of supplies, and almost everything else the family owned. But it was warm and safe.

When the first plentiful harvest of the Plymouth Colony was reaped that autumn, the Pilgrims decided to hold a celebration of thanksgiving. William Bradford, who had become governor when John Carver died, invited the Indians to share in the celebration. Four Pilgrim hunters brought back enough ducks, turkeys, geese, and partridges to last a week. Other settlers brought in clams, fish, and eels.

Cooks spent days making puddings, cornbread, cakes, and preparing vegetables, fruits, and beverages for the coming feast. On the morning of the feast, the Pilgrims were surprised to see Massasoit arrive with ninety of his tribe.

When he realized that the Pilgrims might not have enough food for everyone, Massasoit sent a few of his hunters into the forest. They soon returned with five deer, and venison was added to the feast.

That first Thanksgiving celebration, in October 1621, lasted three days. The settlers and Indians ate and drank, ran races, and had games for the children and adults.

But celebrating Thanksgiving did not become a yearly event in America until long after the Pilgrims had passed into history. For them, Thanksgiving was celebrated only in years with a very good harvest or for some other special reason.

Through good years and bad, the Pilgrims continued to work very hard. Even so, they never became good fishermen, and the London investment company that had sent the Pilgrims to America dissolved without making any profit.

But Plymouth Colony was not a failure. The contributions of the Pilgrims to America were vast. Their system of government set the pattern for the New England town meeting, which sparked a sense of independence in the Colonies.

By establishing a common school for the children of the colony, the Pilgrims introduced the concept of public education for all.

Perhaps most important, the Pilgrims set an example of determination, courage, and firmness in doing what they felt was right. And these qualities helped directly to shape the future of the American Colonies.